BLACK SWIM

BLACK SWIM

poems by
NICHOLAS GOODLY

Copper Canyon Press
Port Townsend, Washington

Cover art: Neka King, *Ocean,* 2021

Copper Canyon Press is in residence at Fort Worden State Park in Port
Townsend, Washington, under the auspices of Centrum. Centrum is a
gathering place for artists and creative thinkers from around the world,
students of all ages and backgrounds, and audiences seeking extraordinary
cultural enrichment.

LIBRARY OF CONGRESS CATALOGING-IN-PUBLICATION DATA
Names: Goodly, Nicholas, author.
Title: Black swim / poems by Nicholas Goodly.
Description: Port Townsend, Washington : Copper Canyon Press, [2022]
| Summary: "A collection of poems by Nicholas Goodly"— Provided by
  publisher.
Identifiers: LCCN 2022017857 (print) | LCCN 2022017858 (ebook)
| ISBN 9781556596513 (paperback) | ISBN 9781619322608 (epub)
Subjects: LCGFT: Poetry.
Classification: LCC PS3607.O56384 B57 2022 (print)
  | LCC PS3607.O56384
  (ebook) | DDC 811/.6—dc23/eng/20220415
LC record available at https://lccn.loc.gov/2022017857
LC ebook record available at https://lccn.loc.gov/2022017858

98765432 FIRST PRINTING

COPPER CANYON PRESS
Post Office Box 271
Port Townsend, Washington 98368
www.coppercanyonpress.org

Acknowledgments

Previous versions of these poems have appeared in the following print and online publications:

Birdcoat Quarterly
Boston Review
Cosmonauts Avenue
Drunk in a Midnight Choir
Gertrude Press
Impakter
Lambda Literary Review
Narrative Magazine
NAUSIKÂE
New South
The New Yorker
Number: Inc
Revisiting the Elegy in the Black Lives Matter Era
wildness

to my blood and chosen family

CONTENTS

BLACK SWIM

I

THE DOWSER

My Black Spell

I breastfed one hunger after another
fear me I know the weight of playthings
the trampoline in the crawl space our family
lost an older sister I am fearless
subtle phoenix older child

there was a time I could bite
and crack into pink jawbreaker
fuck my mouth up into red ants
and explain away the blood in my gums

I've got muscle and am articulate
forged from the hurt parts of the ground
domestic life was child's play
breaking one bone at a time all fun and games
lives in my hands

I could do so much with miniatures
throw the piano into the kitchen attaboy
literally sexual stripped the boys
naked on the lawn I wanted to be
Michelangelo

with Barbie's arched feet or a Bratz
that could bend at the knees there is spit
in my circumstance they call me
unstone they call me unmusic

baby baby baby baby baby voodooed alive
seashell from familial waters
healthy and unimaginably magical
I'm watching your back
best I can baby brother

follow fish follow what runs to us
home licking with gumbo
I do not have words for all the things I desire
In the summer my hair was braided
I am your brother best I can

Don't Look That Witch in the Eye

Mama warned us about that woman.
The whole neighborhood saw she stayed
lonely as an apple core, as if she hoarded
brokenness and it was contagious.

I took the stray mutt
from underneath her shotgun.
I shouldn't have done that.
A bell tolls inside a nearby cathedral.

I keep a straight pin a day, forgive
people easy. I am the mouth
that doesn't go willingly. I am the aftertaste
of rejection. There is not enough healing

in the world to erase, to hold what cannot
be pieced together. Build a church
out of weather, but the sound is already out. I
was the first to seek a way to abandon me.

These days I watch the world
go by and do not breathe life into it.
I am not expected to be anywhere. I can't love
someone cunning into loving me.

This is stonework. My porch a weapon. Its doors
wires and glass, windows unstained with cobweb and lead.
I seek out my own men, roofless, ones without foresight.
And I become the unbearable woman.

Afterwise, or My Father Was Ursa Minor

I am in a house/ with no electricity/ the meat thaws
below/ wings and breasts/ chitterlings and turkey
necks/ undoing themselves/ I stop writing
words/ held up one by one/ to a candlelight/
hold the battery clippers/ tight as a weapon/
aim my grip/ behind my father's ears/ clean
his sober face/ de-toothed and de-clawed/
I've got it now/ his hair/ all over/ gather and brush/
the shame/ from his ribs/ let it flow/ over my palms/
inheritance/ silver herringbone/ worn around the wrist/
there is ice cream/ dripping from the icebox/ I do not
open it/ so as not to spoil the bodies/ and limbs/ preserved
in there/ he is angry about the power/ choiceless/ light
made visible in a web/ no one sees/ father and I/
the bear pit overflowing/ big game/ furbearer/
can't eat the heart/ can't heal it/ father/ look upon
your land/ take the dying grass/ open your jaw/ swallow
father/ feel everything you've missed/ it all remains/
father you stained me/ past the skin/ beaten negro dipper/
lesser chieftain/ we look like each other/ there is nothing
I can do/ about the men/ to be named/ losing their color
in the freezer/ sweating up a storm/ and smelling
rancid through the air/ I can only cut our heads/
father we are not hunting/ the whole of the earth/
sleep/ through the winter/ force of nature/
I already counted/ your fingernails in a jar

Divination

for Big Sister Erin, alive for six hours

when the soul train hesitates
you are there

moving through as if inhibition
never existed already an angel

you would have been a bookkeeper
or arborist there are people who don't come back

held outside our reach
sometimes I can count them

you have two green eyes
Daddy has two green eyes

you would've had the coarsest hair a wolf-girl
your pillows soaked in olive oil

you'd have bullied my bullies
I'd have known the lyrics to Salt-N-Pepa's

"Push It" and we'd have come up
with a tandem dance

I would have fought you
for the last cupcake

the leftover collards are for you
you can have my leg

you would've eaten this world
before I stepped into it

even now I expect a woman to come home
late through the upstairs window

waking Mom to tell her
you're here you snuck out right from her arms

I cannot ask you for much
I see a fire coming miles away

if there is a purpose in this life
let me wash my face in it

Woman among the Electric Flowers

Grandma and I rode in the limo
she kept a pistol her gun
was a pregnant iron garden
it stayed in an old-fashioned bag
full of live wires laces of dandelions
the gator-belly purse lined with honeysuckles
I was nine years old we were in the lead
caravanning carloads of not sunflowers
family to God's house we charged forward
she wore gloves knitted with batteries
and ivy she held her own honeyed veiny hands

the car stopped in the gravel
like a bolt the path to the church
was a static-kissed floor Grandma reached
into her loaded purse and pulled out a white handkerchief
a motionless buzzing lily her fingers tingling she took my palm
careful of her balance she thoughtfully began
her new movements her painstaking body
stained glass and soil bed hummed
like a machine she stepped into Grandpa
his funeral who died of a heart attack

First Poem

I had ever written was about green bug
because I painted one at school or the painting
came later to go with the poem or the poem
was about gold and was printed in rainbow letters
and the painting had a rainbow in it the picture
was a blue watering bucket a butterfly an orange-
and-pink sunset made of vertical stripes
and a purple rainbow and a rose or tulip
and the poem had a refrain it was a song
a song for class or I wrote it for my dance
teacher because she thought I was a poet
and I read it to the class or just to her she said
beautiful or thank you and the painting and poem
are in a frame together now and it matters
that where it all started was a good garden

I Am Coming Home in the Afternoon

from a Tuesday walk and a mild white woman approaches
from underneath a bridge. She appears a blur until
I see a print on her dress. The sketches of slave ships
knocking around her legs—no, the print was fractals.
I grazed a building to make room for her to pass.
If it were slaves, I should've been unmarked.

Inside, the kitchen has shrunk. I boil three eggs that will not fill me up.
I crack their shells and cover them in creole seasonings
like my father—we share a common name—used to do.
I lean on the refrigerator and eat them in no time at all.
Something about the broken bits chucked in the garbage.
Something about the dirty bowl sinking
in the sweltering dishwater, the bubbles
that will pop one after the other.
If it were slaves, I should've been unmarked.

Pride

you call your brother
who you remember
wanting to beat
into the ground almost
a handful of times
and you say
you're coming home
like light he
is up unviolently
when you get home
and you made
a lot of mistakes
and yet you can't hope
for a more
empathetic morning
your brother has known you
his entire delicate life
and he asks
as you open the door
are you ok
yes and you
believe you are at home
and the scar on the home

Darky of the Coven

I was born the color
of the hanged man
I'll give you black
belladonna as a peck on the thumb
a needle fang prick
it slithers in the nail bed

open like a hungry jaw
full of runes and decay
this body creaks
under the skin
overgrown pentacles
through the bone

daggered temperance
lightning in cauldron
and into the stomach
my blood moves thick with angry
stolen hairs my fist heals you too
with blistered reeds

the blacker the berry
the quicker the end
gravity a doll in my hands
gender-fluid recklessness
throwing it round in a circle
making barriers grabbing salt

ancestors torrid-mouthed
summoning fleeting red star
from the swamp queen
over time I want to remember
how it felt yes you remember don't you
call me that name again

this is how we kill each other
a little at a time
a little at a time
breathing green on everything
the smell of a dark lady
the dying of a dark man

II

THE MOON

In some cases
The moon is you

In any case
The moon

JACK KEROUAC

Withdrawal in Drag

Dear pores, squeeze
every venom out of us.
The floorboards are unwell.
Leave no wounds.
Thinly, shapeshifter,
come gaping crow
come broken city.
Practical scaffolding,
temple taking beatings.
Scars, you are now
a giant woman.

Porous Mary, you are longing.
Miss your drink. Lick
grenadine from your claws.
Penitent medusa, eat
a liver every day.
Chew our chances in half.
Change the form of your grit.
Safely trade your ice pick
for a Lisa Frank ice pick.
Become extraordinarily beautiful.
That is your ability. Old phoenix,

last call. Take up
as much room as you need.
Open yourself toward a thing
darker than a person.
Yellow head
soaking through the pillows,
you are made for dissection.
Steady my hand,
the one at your breast,
without blade or precious fire.
I don't want to know you anymore.

Ode to Wearing All My Necklaces at Once

I put them on one at a time
the amethyst and moonstone
little aliens with a broken clip
eighteen-inch smiling robot
bottle cap
jumbo dog chain
rusting owl
all appear magnificent and cold
I lean my head over my lap
and swing their weight
like a hound shaking water
from its coat except carefully
minding its surroundings
they rub against each other
like chiming cats a litter
tangling around themselves
the smell of turning metal
stains my bare neck
Chanel always said take
one accessory off
before walking out the door
before I sleep
I pick my favorite one
and hold on to it
with my good hand
I peel the others off
and put them back on the outside
of my closet where they hang
like bright willow branches
the ropes are together
and the silver chains as well
the meaty ones scratch
and rattle in their place
the whole gold set is like pennies

syruping down the wall
before I flip the light switch
lying underneath the comforter
my thumbs work the last piece over
like flies to sugar
until they tire

Lipsticks

OVAH No. 5
Not That Innocent Pink
Violet Chachki
See You Next Tuesday
Amanda Lepore's Revenge
Nude Descending a Staircase
They're All Gonna Laugh at You
I Will Always Love Blue
This Is My Hair
Electric Twiggy
Grey Gardens
NeNe Is Very Rich Green
Spell on You
A Clair Huxtable Hue
The Night the Lights Went Out in Georgia
Mutha! Has Arrived
Lips Don't Lie
Put a Little Yellow in My Bowl
Mrs. Bates
Priscilla, Green of the Desert
Bag Lady Blue
Metallic Cindi Mayweather
Little Latin Boy in Drag
Touch All This Skin
Orange in the 212
Burnt Sunset Blvd
Iris Apfel Bloom
Naomi's Pout
C'est Si Bon
Meow
Fleetwood Matte
Divine Intervention
Good Witch, Bad Witch
Onyx First Lady
Proud Mary
The Banana-52's

Cleopatra
Rupacalypse Red
No Wire Hangers
Beat for the Gods
Barbarella Blue
Bette Davis Eyes
Opulence
Tangerine

Mother, I'm Confusing Myself with My Surroundings Again

Lock the door like a mouth behind you
get warm and again comfortable
stomp and shed your boots on my shag
say no to *don't I feel good inside*
I wore everything on me for you

a naked back is at work in a field of mirror
my lungs are turning the ceiling round in blades
that sweep the room like pieces of finger
all of my poems and windows are gathered
for the opening of a decent body

I'm gonna kick the bucket one day
and you're gonna wish you'd kept spooning me
say you want a raspberry say you want a bloodsucker
I made presents I made you a sheet of broken glass

I want the dust from your clothes
to collect into a man
let *me* against *you* mean *a potent home*
let it knock you out
let me lick you dead and here
it would not be hard
I want to shoot between your teeth

the front door is on fire
and weighs 180 pounds
fuck my closet right in the leopard
and what a domestic orgasm
if you are here it's how I called you

Nudes

call them low art I send bangers only
my nudes are a Rothko *Yellowbone No. 2* I am
pictured in pleasure a joy almost aggressive
I am the halo around everything
and still go unnoticed

my nudes are dripping maple
portraits of stiff flower crowns
I capture a cool garden image
and freckles in Coltrane rhythm
and it tears the boys apart

I flash unbeat thunder of mountains unmounted
torso bare and off the evening news my family
jewels not cropped into an obituary no candlelight
vigil holding poses in my bathroom mirror
all of Earth in a dream

red-light magician photographing
a cocky thicc watermelon queer
tasteful butter queen
endowed blue demoness
I am the Laura Palmer of my friend group

serving rich ebony courses between
the sexes sissy drops
his towel softboy well-lit softie looks
like a hanging black man fairy on a blanket
my little flavor my fat memory

I appear opened and shared unasked for
and free my nudes are documents proofs of miracle
the branded stallion has set the barn on fire
black spectacle shot on film and still living

Wet Man

I will make my own man
I will stitch together a coat of drunk minks
until he my man is drunk in his collar
and wearing a sharp biting harness my man
is drunk with his nose in his collar

I want to wear gold-stick appendages
Partner my man lend me your saber-toothed legs
your big sleeve we should have children
we should dress these children in this single pair
of fishnets we will see to it these fishnets
kick their legs in a Georgia river

my man will take a handful of my nipple
he my man will *cheers* to cocoa butter
all ten fingers will see to it
and the dandelion oil he my man
my man has ten seeing fingers
his ten dandelion fingers
will see to my nipple

and nothing is embarrassing
he will snore like a man
who is asleep and happy
if I want to wear him I wake him
I will let myself in as he yawns
river my main man
rivers are drooling tongues

the South is wet sweet vinegar
river let us spell each other's names
with the fewest letters
just like that and nothing else until a poem
I wish I had a blind tongue
I wish I was stupid and naive in the mouth
I wish I had a blind tongue

Lyrics for Sex over TV Dinners

it starts with a taste for lumens
a fix for captivation
I think the world of you
and the show *Horace and Pete*

your mouth is a bad strawberry
I'll never fuck a grizzly quite like you
and still want to swallow whole
big black-souled canary

this refrain grinds its teeth
with all the bravado
of the last American buffalo
this refrain was a virgin

we've been in each other's bodies
what lucky boys we are
no one owns each other all the way

these memories keep their eyes on you
bees rub themselves into lovemaking music
and no one talks

about Jessica Lange to me like you do
all my cells cum when you say *American*
say it from my toes to my chin make it mean *timeless*
in your unsuspecting body

anything is fun until it isn't
the we of it all is weaving into your head
like worms loving you to pieces
loving you loving you to to pieces pieces

Mail-Order Bride: Judy

His human-sized wooden package waited for him
in the empty corner of his loft.
She's arrived! In all her glory
packed in polystyrene peanuts!

Her profile:

How exciting you are concerned about me. I am lucky.
If you could you would rest your head in your own lap.
I was married eight years ago but died on impact. After,
I was originally lonely. Unleavable me. And then there
was that season. Earned me several burns. Making the bed
cures an unmade bed. I would like to forget and you
are here concerned about me. I am looking for a man
who believes in everything from chewing to star. You
have seen precisely what your body can do. Watch moon?
Is she full? Is she sexy? I trust you know how to have me.
If you could how fearfully would you kiss your own cheek?

With love in his heart,
he grabbed a crowbar, cracked open the box,
and out leaped a hundred singing grasshoppers.

sweet nothings[1]

1. you look so strong you're so lucky you guys don't even have to work out I bet you don't even try for that body is it true what they say about you guys? I bet you would wear me out damn that ass you gotta be mixed with something nice ass yall all got those big asses hey. HEY! mm–hmm damn that ass what a cute nose where you from? I been struck with jungle fever lately I wouldn't want you to rob me ha ha yo you Puerto Rican? you Pwaairto Reeken? you from an island, huh. you Egyptian? you're so cute you can't be all black, right? I bet you would never date a black guy bet you never been with a white guy before what that ass do what those lips of yours do? the things you would do to me ooh I can tell you're trouble the things I would do to you

.

Elephants on Roses

I took a saucer of tomato
slices, glittered in sea salt,
into bed, ate them pristine
from my knees. His erection
a tusk as he snored. This
is what pain sounds like:
We are dragging a bronze bell.

Melancholia

there is that one restlessness
he wakes up from a nightmare
pulls you close

hail beats the serious earth
everyone else seems unabashedly held
who makes the soul anyway?

then there is the one unsleep
you are the most worst thing in the room
and both of you won't say it

and then the world tastes
so much like a lemon
no more rhythm or blues
when lightning strikes the dog

Your Amazon.com order "Latex Canine Mask-Teal" has shipped!

sensitive feet
tongued down
damn two
of a kind
mouth waters
my appetite
grown
I wear
oxblood
collar
steeled
fashioned plow
you don't
want me
it's written
all over
your saliva
good
boy speak
I bow
and wow
then it
is over
a fool
ain't learned
a thing
a man
becomes a
chair
this world
becomes a
traditional color
when you
allow it
to end

R&B Facts

All mermaids are black
and only hunt sailor men
who talk that fucknoise

Egypt is the proud grandmother
of Harlem and she sits back in her chair
with a switch in her hand

There is a brother
and a sister somewhere
just right for every child

If we didn't murder black boys
we would have voices that speak in song
and the music we'd make would birth storms

We all can walk on water
as long as we never said
no antiblack shit

If we lit a candle for every pain
hurled toward trans folk
whole planets would be up in smoke

If we planted a tree for every word
against women the ground
would lose sight of the sun

A dead child's name at the top of your lungs
like an earth-splitting lightning rod
has the power to remember them back

One in three black girls learns
to swim by being chased away from
the shallow end of a brown community pool

Two out of five black families know
death as that play cousin who sleeps over
under comforters on the living room floor

There are black hills that only grow
in the heat of the sun
made of thick curling hair

The ghosts of black slaves are waiting
in one big front room with good music
till their whole families are free

Melanin, it's been proven,
has endured more than any beam of steel

The Greek goddess of peaceful resistance
has died in a long-burning fire
and is buried in a fruitless urn

Nina Simone was born
in the fifteenth century her crib
was the bottom of a full boat

The bigger the hoops
the braver the body

Armpit hair is permanently sexy
acrylic nails start fires
in a heavy heart

Melanin bleeds a softness
wetter than silk

No one survives Etta James

The strongest homes are built
on onyx brick on muscle
covered in charcoal skin

Melanin is a blessing
gold melting in our hands

Melanin is light on every
surface of the day

There is no color on Earth
that is not some child's favorite

If every human stood shoulder to shoulder
we would make an iron castle
with beating veins between the walls

All of us lying head to head
is a river feeding an ocean
too black to swim

The Empress

i.m. Bessie Smith, "Empress of the Blues" (1894–1937)

i.m. Robert Hayden (1913–1980)

mourn proud
wailing Venus
unslaughtered flame
you've outgrown your angels
mammy of black keys
your blackness pools

opens the sky
the stars are well nurtured
and shine like reparations
dark and serious upon you
ain't a silver moon
that isn't yours

the *say it loud!*
prolific scorched earth
provider of sins
your pain takes up a voice
roaring sound of blue
sure as you're born

the devil's gonna git you
light that asks to know light
what else do you have
to promise God?
what more
can he owe you?

are you any good?
black hair
the teeth of song
dangerous female galaxy
the devil's gonna git you
heart and soul and all

Negro as Lighthouse

permanent and steel
my breath is stubborn
I am thinking
of an image for failure
a garden of rocks
it doesn't take much to live
I don't stand
against fog and night
how long have we
been here before
been brave
and worried
gulls slice the air
in two even pieces
drunken artists walk
like waking children
wiping their eyes
clear as fishbowls
this one is drawing
the same image
of the gardener's hands
over and over
until it is perfect
I collect his discarded papers
and pile the flimsy things
into a tall stack
feeble as the artist himself

Black Mecca

Magic city little trap
you are a mess of tonguing brass
a lap of slack jaws open in your wake
as fire boys jive in your sugarcane song
a coat of muddy lard thickens the air
every crevice on our bodies is wet
the nights are purple and dutifully leaning

The way we slow is growing tasteless and we
are chasing the perfect catfish we are go-
ing for the birthday candle dragonfly
you keep with your flower bodies and stink
I want you to be as mean as jasper
and we are chewing shards of lapis and
one thing wants another and everything stays

One thing wants another and everything stays
repeat after me repeat after me
how sweet and vulgar and backward
and heat a flame robe eats you
here it comes take a whiff
of your bubbling nose we
are in here together a black peach pie

Let's hear it for the bitters
in drink and in men for the men
like doors that smile and open
for the ones with hot garnet in their veins
let's go back to my place there is an oven
I call home lay me on a sapphire grill
tell me you can taste the lovin'

Tell me you can taste the lovin'
as much as the street is pavement look
how it's made us an inevitable beam
the streetlights outweigh the stardrip I am
learning to say the alphabet in confidence
I remember those days as lined sleek socks

You are no pelican
you've been my place for cooking men
children are squirming in your pores
you are a home for amethyst dogs
what a thing to witness magnolia petals
storm the streets like ferocious pearl swans
their pretty blindness their cooing snare

Confessional

I ask a Magic 8 Ball if Jesus is real
poetry is untelling a lie
I smile when my friends have bad news
I try to leave something beyond repair
in every sacred space
candlewick and chalice
the moths close their wings
I watch hours of brothers
and sisters slamming their fists
into one another
some days I wish I was both of them
I want to roughen up souls
yank a fistful of someone's hair
I drank like hell the night
before the funeral Thundercat
is a poem so is bad drag
I am drawn to people
who deserve me the least
I could easily be a worse person
how many people am I
and where is the body
I crave hung poems here is a bird
in an airport I have wet dreams
that end in cold blood I order a man
to kneel for my affection
and he does it oh boy
am I capable of sweet heart
I am good at the yoke
I have sympathy
once I heard a man say *nigger*
and wanted him to mean *me*
a poem doesn't have to mean anything
a poem is a fire with no end
if given another chance in this life
I'd make peace with getting weaker every day
I ask God to come inside me

God opens his mouth
and creates the sky
waves of old cold stars
a poem sharpens the wind
everything is true
I need to be told what to believe

III

TO YOU WHO FIT THE DESCRIPTION

To You Who Fit the Description

My ugly lion, people are remarkably cruel
to one another. There is no one to blame.
Things die all the time and still
you do not. You force the sun
to grow fiercer from your hard pastel
dribbling sound. Your hands
are innocent as you, a domestic earthquake
taking in families and emerald water.

Chocolate moaner, you are a perfect decade.
You are an ape. I can just see
the colored lips all over you.
Lips like wet diseases, clinking vertebrae
in the day's full belly. What happens then?
Street whale, city body, you are woke,
critter-eating, inhaling little artful bodies
like ice cream. You don't speak for the gods.
May our wrongs create trouble.

To You Who Fit the Description

My violent love, what big teeth you have.
Follow dark meat and dead ends. I choose you
as my brother. I take you, pretty
man-killer. My colt boy, who was the first
to taste you? I want to taste like apples
wet with black rain. I wish I was better
at facing you naked. I want to suck
your thumb and mine till they are white
as our palms, but they taste like blood
and yours taste like mine. Make me
as I see you—a well of dull history,
a wealth of pain. Put your dirty
face against my dirty face.

Don't blame yourself. You don't
sound unimportant. Break our noses
on my guilty brain. And then comes
tomorrow. I am a chain away from
what I feel. Heartache leaves
both of us running. Your last meal
you pick us down to the gristle.
Remember me.

To You Who Fit the Description

My careful sibling, hear me speaking pearls
pulling them in strings
from my mouth.
Hear them break
across my gums,
patience-formed, heavy.

Close your ears to the loud stones.
You have a goldfish swimming in your belly.
The sun is loud and new in your breast.
Peppermint men are playing cards on your breath.
You're growing yellow moss for hair.
Land mines sleep in your eyes.
Your skin is wrapping paper held with taut twine.
My dear, the rocks feel it beneath you.
Growing.

Pinch your stomach, a soft, warm pillow.
You're not dead yet—not even close.
Save those tears, clean and fresh as ginger.
You primal thing,
tiptoeing, hushed, picked still young.
You're a stag sprinting across the ocean floor.
You're a lionfish swimming in midair.
Think of your big bones, your wide back.
It is the year of the beast of burden.

To You Who Fit the Description

My tired fighter, malice finds you
like wasps, follows you into the pavement.
You could've lived.
You yelled too loud, too often.
Guns fire amber at you and you
stand there enormous and perfect.

On the ground, you find yourself humbled.
You unfurl a long scarlet ribbon.
My pleas won't pull you back.
We were only ever human.
This ending is a good one.
Your body sent home, safe.
I prayed the wax down to a dry puddle.
There's not enough energy to bury you.
You were a king first.

To You Who Fit the Description

My strongest hand, the bond
between us, there is no losing it. Tomorrow
will happen, innocent as a white word. I'm not
scared of anything anymore. We are heavy
and imaginary, an unspoken train. Tomorrow
barrels out from the relentless concrete ground.
We forget our fate and build ourselves a heaven.

To You Who Fit the Description

To you who fit the description,
look at what time has done to us. There
is a furnace under every night. Inherit the house.
There are mountains in your name. The land
is ready and the wind is real.
We will be soft-shell and unbreakable.
We will never tire. Our mothers are alive
beneath our skin. Come into the light, Goliath.
Release one pain. We are the masters
of that good summer, sun-built and deathless.

IV

BLACK ART

Black Art

speak dead blacks
my mouth needs
learning from the best blues
a douse of fire there
all along
a thirst
this small sadness
inherent
between my ears
I ask of the grave
what I ask of the light
how it reveals
the noiselessness
of skin how it keeps
no poison
there is time
to lay it bare
whimsical and with no meat
worked through
until nothing
a rainstorm
the heavens soak
my uncaring socks
this means everything
I am a dowser
begging the water
I told you
from the start
if I do this
you have to take
care of it

Floromancy

You convince yourself you are attracted
to men with shedding husk hair, swollen
and gurgling bellies, meals of walk-on-by
and midnight train, coffee teeth packed
with meat and popcorn kernels.

You offer a candy-apple-red glove caught
in the grates of a rain-filled gutter, a staggering
white folded airplane, your missing tooth
and an extra rib, a handful of the smell of wet straw.

You ask for a lover to call you *salty baby*
while his wire-fence hands squeeze your ass. As he breathes
tobacco and vanilla into your lungs, you commit yourself
to naming his chest hairs. His arm a cut and tattered pillow,
his skin paper tigers in your mouth.

You lay down a rat king to take his side
of the bed, let many times sweetener in with snakes.
Yours or his old-laid spunk crystallizes Pop Rocks,
a frosted grave streaming along a wall.

You want a home in a butterfly garden
where the McGuire Sisters sing. A song that should be
for you, you will dedicate to someone else. You envelop
dangerous thoughts like cups of sour milk. A prayer
slides down your throat, forgiveness in cold gulps
from inside out. You feel no need for penance
until you do. On the first night, you fall asleep kissing
scabs and everything about his face is real.

Seeing a Lavender Octopus with Large Stag Antlers

She brings her starved limbs to you.
One arm grabs hold of her gold-leafed horns,

rubs the sensitive shapes until they chip. She keeps
three hearts underground boiling in sacred warm-blooded rhythm.

One arm wants to devour
your muscled form, sifts through your abdomen

built for soft sciences. Her brain is fast
as downhill smoke, a delicious movement of angel

in frantic pink wind. She coos *write a drowning poem.*
It is the season for boy trust fall and flickering candle.

You are a happy suckling catfish inside a den of ribs.
You are captured now, without your knowing.

One arm turns slick glass pearl into sucked plum and seared peach.
Another unravels raw grace, gentle, small and singing

like an unclenching fist. You both are drunk from the glowing reek
of each other, moon bouquet and empty honey. She speaks
 in night voice

about obsidian and cloud therapy. She remembers
the face of her shore.

She wets the bed and floor with every tendril and fiber
of her head, one arm opening to the pleas of water grass.

She is still all this time hungry. She is jealous
of the softness of your sex. You give in, dive into her,

one arm fragile as bathwater. You are eaten. You both look
at the blank walls. She is unsatisfied and thankful for fire.

You stand to get a glass of water from the bathroom. You
look in the mirror. As the liquid pools through you, it rains as
 you swallow.

Grief

you already fell
you give her
your young tongue
every week
you tell her
your new favorite animal
today black jaguar quick
as any life
this week she will say
black jaguar
slobbering
borealis eyes
crossing rivers
stalk and paddle
the best animal for you
how you must've
put time
into that animal
thought it out so well
the slightest sound
and you bolt upright

you memorize pallbearers
she offers the challenges
of a meadow
you list all the ethers
she plays
an unforgiving hand
blessed or otherwise
you hear noises
and you run
strawberry thief
all at once
she has robbed you
of your feelings
you cannot find
a crack in the wall

give way to poison
she devours
what you buried
Warren
your dear
jungle cat

Race Play and the Joy of Painting

this is excellent work
and we'll fill it up just like so
blend it so everything is soft
chains around your neck
shadows in the snow
we don't use any patterns
we just let it happen
I just like to wipe the whip
titanium white
outward outward outward
back to the good days
time to start making some big decisions here
darkest kinks
a touch of cadmium
two hairs and some air
that will be our light source
light bending over
until it cannot recover
very gentle quiet belt
get it out my system
push them right into the sun
one off
take the Prussian black
you can still make a mistake
that's all it takes
kiss every inch
don't know where it goes
don't know if we care
noose play
good answer
only a man
barely that
royal majesty
on top of the black gesso
way up high in the mountains
liquid white

drop color in the sky
so it's not just flat and dead
let's have some fun
and beat the devil out of it

How We Sleep at Night

Our backs like canvases
face each other.
We tug at a blanket.
The fan hums and clicks
above our heads.
I sigh,
Oh God.
He stirs.

What about God?

Nothing. Sleep.

In the bathroom
like clattering living jewels
an unmistakable hand
crawls from the faucet, skitters
into the bedroom, tugs
its way like a slow and heavy monster
onto the bed. Into my ear it carves with a talon.

Your baby's breath is coming in this year
and will die particularly fast.

Considering Another Roach by the Shower Drain

He is the size of brown leather scrap,
waving wires like flags above his head. I assess,
gather my nerve, and settle to hold
a new thirty-two-ounce bottle of bleach.

From outside the door, a spritz
into the cramped room. Tenacious and sick,
he will stir, and then what? My conviction is slow.
Some days I am more fidgets than man.

A spray and here he comes scuttling along the wall. I spray
on the walls until the walls are melting and when he falls
my trigger follows him with heavy chemical puddles.
Underneath a broken tile *I've got you now.*

I twist off the nozzle and pour, pour until he floats flooded
out with the wet, gray floor-scum on his back, a dead bulldog.
The last hefty words of the bleach circle all three drains
in the apartment for self-defense. The air is clean-toxic

and I am coughing-red-lung happy
because I didn't have to touch him at all,
not even once, and if I had, he would've been spotless.
If he were I, he would do what I did.

Scorpio and Pisces

I am
colorless
romantic viper
divinely limbed
crawling dandelion
weighed with
necessary
evil
poison
I can cleanse
you incredibly
do you think
I is dangerous?
you answer
wide mouthed
a reply
round as glass
plunge both hands
into God
paternal blood
escapes your mouth
you are between spirits
not on fire
and gill
this is a love
with no teeth
we each other's
axe sweat
and embarrassed sky
you won't do
and the water
not fine
follow me down
to whenever
I am most afraid
the color
of the water
rarely seen at all
rivermouth
scent of dead
woods
with the clean things

hungry hook
in your open jaw
reach me
something
chokes
this is not
the when to act
clear room
tame yourself
for living
cannot be rushed
beneath ground
it is not alone
it is not a grave
holey fungi
we were made
for each other
another word
for *deep*
salacious sex
moving
burping water
no trouble
no trouble until
a storm
unravels nature
was it a ghost?
was it fun?
then I am jealous
I am sporing
birthmarks
dwelling places
on forest floor
where everyone
was whole
rosewater devil
the two of us
bleed
the sunrise
on the water's surface
I am leaving
bruises in waves

Daisies

We wanted this: to grow domestic Ferris-wheeled children
and to bloom liver spots on our skin like faded badges.

I had that dream again where I lived forever
and spat up silver petals, fashioning them into a shield.
You were a woman and the nurses bludgeoned you to death.

You wake to me with a long sad tail.
My kisses are believable. My mistress
is the rain on the apricots.

Three of Swords

times like these
I know my heart
a drum in a second line
I love you intelligently
I believe in cherry
hard candies
a glimpse at heaven
where kind things
learn their kindness
I am convinced of you
at the center of it
pink with color
the present is irreplaceable
wear three million feathers
I say *ooo wee*
when I get excited
so happy it makes a sound
I hold you
under the surface
I love you inchly
you know where
to put the dishes
you know how
to love the dog's speckled tummy
you can count how many steps
to the door
and you stay
after all this time
wonderful man
may you always
empty of violence
I am yours
yes
I want to live
ooo wee
just wonderful

Aaron with the flat butt. thin. not a good dancer.

after francine j. harris

I wake up early the bed to myself reach
for my privates out of lotion so I use spit

your tooth is chipped skin is pale I am not as fetching
as you my ass stretch marked stomach hyperpigmented

I keep my socks on one of my nail beds bruised
you have masculine dairy feet my voice is low and feminine

I am tranquilizer the first draft of a masterpiece I hated you
from the first time I saw you at Mary's afraid to dance

back then bad at everything but still you are wanted I am diva
    I twerk joints
overextended and lip-sync every song precisely and I am found
    disgraceful

these gays don't know what they want these hoes ain't loyal
so they settle on you I like to think there was a time

when I was the ace boon coonz
I lie to myself about this while you take your pick

of what I think I am owed your knees are weird
I have a mint plant it grows how it should unless

I overwater the thing then it spreads its loud flavors
all over I suffocate on its crispness you Trojan horse

of an herb you've run my smelling wild
you lack subtlety you are ever only spring

not one bald spot on your head I am aging
one of these boys is going to break your heart

so bad you can't get it up anymore
that you must apologize make excuses for your inadequacies

that you can only masturbate to the thought
of getting it stiff from your rival

that you only come to him degrading you
shrinking you down to a watermelon seed

you will think you deserve it this way you and your full head
of awful hair that everyone finds so damn sexy

cherub and lanky Apollo I have nothing
but style over you you are six feet tall

I bet they're only just saying they're in love
with you they don't really mean it

says he needs you you're all
he ever thinks about

this one calls you beautiful
he is beautiful himself

he says he can't live without you
you feel the same and say it

I envy you still
believing each other

"Love Is a Battlefield" by Pat Benatar

when you put yours to my face
it smells like a scentless eight-foot iris
the things I let get put inside me are contagious

and a beauty the things I let get put inside me are sick
a silky purr grinding full moon loving itself brutal
in this version I didn't fuck it up but healed you

I didn't birth the worst in your sensitive tummy
we would make a garden of blessed starfish
breathing in and all the way innocently out

I still love naming you sensible names
cold water bugs I name you white ticklish toes
myself I name the new gray beauty

I am constantly a sick cat in heat you believe
I am trying hard believe I am still warm in your palm
until you finally bite in are you hot yet?

we are a waltz crawling content on the floor
we are a tenor too perfectly in the middle of things
both hysterical men both staying innocent together

we are always that time at the beach house
we will always need each other the most
and I will never not at all let you kill a thing

Siren

Each night I peel back
every iridescent scale
for a mound of flesh
I can agree with.
I am something that looks
like it glows in the dark
but doesn't.
These shells are plastered on
as breasts. My hair parades
as horses. I refuse
my sunken name
and sing to a body
I want for myself.
I will show you
how to burn
dry lavender sprigs.
I can teach you
how to clench
your teeth until
your forebears bleed.
It couldn't matter
anything
to you, could it? Listen
to the woodchipper.
I scrape my webbed fingers
against coral
until the tendons
between them snap free.
I masturbate
my thudding fin
against a tangle of eel.
Make me come
air or lightning.
I have yet to touch

every part of my body.
I am waiting
in every pan of steam
until you return
as big in your body
as you've ever been.

Scrying

Now if your heart was as big as your mouth, you'd be real

DMX

nine dogs
from the water
this means something
if you want it to
forgive the bones
in your psychic
womb of a mouth
clairvoyant sets of
crystal fang
mercy is inevitable
let *the dogs*
mean *the water*
intuitive ripple
mercy is a womb
intelligent dark animal
brilliant shattering teeth
healing is persistent
as you need it to be
fuck penance
its canine obedience
and stalking gait
let your angel
off the leash
be the damned thing
then set the damned
thing free
finally the water
the smell
of divinity
silvering sky

and wet skin
pure howling heart
there is no one
left to hide
mercy has a shadow
you ask the moon
for your reflection
she gives you
her last breath

Airs Aboveground

I call for birds and the Lord
no birds come

I am thirsty at the gates
sip the floodwater

the rope was for a tire swing
my shadow hangs

like a wound
on the tree trunk

oh Lord the things
I was bound to do

sometimes I think
I know you

if you hear me
do not leave me

forget what I've given the earth
the sin I've shared

I am a morsel of what I am
unable to run from anything

and where are we now?
oh the sound

of the white side
of railroads

I am close to the sun
these are the pitfalls

I still belong to you
I come alive with lightning scars

I choose I choose I choose
death by horse by horse

Southern Comfort

for Matt J. Jones, MonteQarlo, and Kiwan Benson

back then darkness
  couldn't touch us

we were christened
  in soul power

fish jumped
  toward the sun

like boys
  out of coffins

named house flowers
  Eartha and Grace

magnanimous swell
  devout shore

cancer and water
  around their throats

gone all at once
  the light in this world

there is life in yellow fields
  breathing thin as gossamer

back then
  we were immortal

naked
  unsinkable

our heads
  up

bobbing
  curly-headed apples

hands in the air
  ringing amen

Self-Portrait as Ocean Bed

I don't deserve
second chances
a sinking ship
an empty cup
wading in
its name
lyric vessel
held together
by miracle

Isn't it terrible
to have faith
like that
crackable
as a soap dish
I remember
not needing
to come up for air
it was spectacle
and breathtaking
insurmountable
oil spill
that drag
beneath sand
just when I think
there is enough
then there is
a hole in it

Who would claim
this ineffective
home the walls still
mourning I see
uninspiring salt
a blackness ahead
where nothing escapes
wouldn't it be nice
to die only once

Transubstantiation with Pumpernickel

When I quit my hardheaded body, gut me
like a deer and stuff me with hundred-dollar bills.
Present me my most unapologetic,
indifferent river ripping through a country.
I get away with it. Heaven looks white
as chicken bone. Peach soda blood of life
through blueberry Sour Punch Straws,
this is how I remix the altar
and make my anointing to taste.
Unsew the minks lining my casket.
Pick up their scurrying souls and lay them
flourishingly on our Savior's coat.
If you love someone,

tell them. The rain cloud heads home.
Then God will give me his real name.
Johmarcus Johmarcus Johmarcus,
he repeats in my breast. Most mountains
are soundless. I will never sleep here.
I'll get a grill with his name in diamonds.
Father wakes his own. I remember
cypress trees. My name tattooed across his heart,
this is how we learn each other.
Everybody prays. When nothing
is wrong in ordinary moments,
I let the light look for its children.
You are free to save yourself.

Hypersigil

I claim myself apparition
in pieces overgrown and wicked
all shade and stones
I am ghost-making
the soul floats
sad wood in crowded sea
the weight of a forest
Lord we heard you
in our own way
there is no meaning
in all these knowledges
shrinking combustible light
the waves kiss the shore
softly over and softly over
the night drinks it in
the viewer and the view
enough to let angels
one night after the other
I was born your tongue
meant for divining
I've done every person blood
I used to want big wings
this affectionate voice
this cold underground
black ice says only the kindest things
I don't know how to mourn that way
how to sing it if it isn't real
tell me how I deserve it
won't nobody else
where have I placed
your magnificent heart?
the baby's tears are quieting
what shall I do? your answer
softly over and softly over

Evening Prayer

who bestowed upon me
this habit of wanting
music from a pen this addiction
to the gentleness of vowels
what are these notes
from people's heads
what is the point
of being the last one
to speak a beautiful language
I am a fraction
of what I could've been
what else can I contribute
I am outdone by children
with more to lose
a teenager instructing me
how to breathe
these kids are quick
they grab the hands
of their neighbors
pull each other
safely up for air
there is your enemy and son
your wife and brother
your prize and secret cross
golden fleece and weighted cast
heaven knows
I want this to be a poem
people reach for
how often have I told myself
I am not strong and time
keeps proving me wrong
when snow doesn't come
when I am not enough
let me do the right thing
and make a rope of words

let it begin with me even now
there is richness beyond belief
vulnerable warrior what risk is there
we who already die in so many places
this not even the worst of them
no one line is revolutionary
no one word ever is
I am grateful for not dying yet
I inhale what is in front of me
everything is changing
young hearts any love
I can describe for you
does not suffice but you
are worth my every effort
one day you will know love like this
and write it better than I

Voices and Organs Playing Loudly

I got a recipe for geranium eyes
I got the hookup for kerosene hands
hallelujah! out of your bodies
get a hallelujah! straight out
of your body get into some brave
stretch-marked skin around the armpit
make it tiger skin get into a long pubic hair
at the crevice of the groin, eel-slick and erect

I got a craving for a knight and a bath
the days add up to why-me-Lord birds
the evenings is a big why-be gorilla
I've been thinking in black-bone hours, Lord
I've been thinking of you in a trunk chest, Lord
I have an open mouth full of kingless crowns
I remember one specific whipping
and I remember forgiving hard
my whole father and my whole mother

I've worn beautiful and ordinary white dresses
we wore them together, Lord
forgive me very much
I have a whistle like the devil's
I am collecting the people's ears
excuse me in the meantime
make at least my shadow a good man
Lord, were you for me or someone else?

About the Author

Nicholas Goodly is a writer and artist living in Atlanta, Georgia. They are the writing editor for *Wussy Magazine,* a Cave Canem fellow, and a team member of the performing arts platform Fly on a Wall. Nicholas received an MFA and a teaching fellowship from Columbia University and is the recipient of the 2017 Poetry Society of America Chapbook Fellowship. Nicholas is currently a PhD student in creative writing at Florida State University.

Lannan Literary Selections

For two decades Lannan Foundation has supported the publication and distribution of exceptional literary works. Copper Canyon Press gratefully acknowledges their support.

LANNAN LITERARY SELECTIONS 2022

Chris Abani, *Smoking the Bible*

Victoria Chang, *The Trees Witness Everything*

Nicholas Goodly, *Black Swim*

Dana Levin, *Now Do You Know Where You Are*

Michael Wasson, *Swallowed Light*

RECENT LANNAN LITERARY SELECTIONS FROM COPPER CANYON PRESS

Mark Bibbins, *13th Balloon*

Sherwin Bitsui, *Dissolve*

Jericho Brown, *The Tradition*

Victoria Chang, *Obit*

Leila Chatti, *Deluge*

Shangyang Fang, *Burying the Mountain*

June Jordan, *The Essential June Jordan*

Laura Kasischke, *Lightning Falls in Love*

Deborah Landau, *Soft Targets*

Rachel McKibbens, *blud*

Philip Metres, *Shrapnel Maps*

Aimee Nezhukumatathil, *Oceanic*

Paisley Rekdal, *Nightingale*

Natalie Scenters-Zapico, *Lima :: Limón*

Natalie Shapero, *Popular Longing*

Frank Stanford, *What About This: Collected Poems of Frank Stanford*

Arthur Sze, *The Glass Constellation: New and Collected Poems*

Fernando Valverde, *America* (translated by Carolyn Forché)

Matthew Zapruder, *Father's Day*

Poetry is vital to language and living. Since 1972, Copper Canyon Press has published extraordinary poetry from around the world to engage the imaginations and intellects of readers, writers, booksellers, librarians, teachers, students, and donors.

COPPER CANYON PRESS WISHES TO EXTEND A SPECIAL THANKS TO THE FOLLOW-
ING SUPPORTERS WHO PROVIDED FUNDING DURING THE COVID-19 PANDEMIC:

4Culture
Academy of American Poets (Literary Relief Fund)
City of Seattle Office of Arts & Culture
Community of Literary Magazines and Presses (Literary Relief Fund)
Economic Development Council of Jefferson County
National Book Foundation (Literary Relief Fund)
Poetry Foundation
U.S. Department of the Treasury Payroll Protection Program

WE ARE GRATEFUL FOR THE MAJOR SUPPORT PROVIDED BY:

TO LEARN MORE ABOUT UNDERWRITING
COPPER CANYON PRESS TITLES,
PLEASE CALL 360-385-4925 EXT. 103

WE ARE GRATEFUL FOR THE MAJOR SUPPORT PROVIDED BY:

Richard Andrews

Anonymous (3)

Jill Baker and Jeffrey Bishop

Anne and Geoffrey Barker

In honor of Ida Bauer, Betsy
  Gifford, and Beverly Sachar

Donna Bellew

Matthew Bellew

Sarah Bird

Will Blythe

John Branch

Diana Broze

John R. Cahill

Sarah Cavanaugh

Stephanie Ellis-Smith and
  Douglas Smith

Austin Evans

Saramel Evans

Mimi Gardner Gates

Gull Industries Inc. on behalf of
  William True

The Trust of Warren A. Gummow

William R. Hearst III

Carolyn and Robert Hedin

David and Jane Hibbard

Bruce Kahn

Phil Kovacevich and Eric Wechsler

Lakeside Industries Inc. on behalf
  of Jeanne Marie Lee

Maureen Lee and Mark Busto

Peter Lewis and Johnna Turiano

Ellie Mathews and Carl Youngmann
  as The North Press

Larry Mawby and Lois Bahle

Hank and Liesel Meijer

Jack Nicholson

Gregg Orr

Petunia Charitable Fund and
  adviser Elizabeth Hebert

Suzanne Rapp and Mark Hamilton

Adam and Lynn Rauch

Emily and Dan Raymond

Joseph C. Roberts

Jill and Bill Ruckelshaus

Cynthia Sears

Kim and Jeff Seely

Joan F. Woods

Barbara and Charles Wright

In honor of C.D. Wright,
  from Forrest Gander

Caleb Young as C. Young Creative

The dedicated interns and
  faithful volunteers of
  Copper Canyon Press

The Chinese character for poetry is made up of two parts:
"word" and "temple." It also serves as pressmark for
Copper Canyon Press.

The poems are set in Interstate Compressed and Bembo Std.
Book design by Becca Fox Design.